STILT WALKING
AT
MIDNIGHT

STILT WALKING
AT
MIDNIGHT

poems by

J. Esmé Jel'enedra

Hummingbird Press
Santa Cruz, California

Copyright © 2004 by Jonell Esmé Jel'enedra

All Rights Reserved.

Library of Congress Control Number: 2004101918
ISBN: 0-9176373-7-7

Grateful acknowledgement is made to the following publications in which some of these poems first appeared: *Ally*, *Porter Gulch Review*, *Quarry West*, *The Bathyspheric Review*, and *Writing for Our Lives*.

Cover art: Sandra England.
Design and layout assistance: Ken Weisner
Cover design: Stuart Spencer Smith
www.badgerdogg.com
Photo of the author by Stuart Spencer Smith

Hummingbird Press
2299 Mattison Lane
Santa Cruz, CA 95062-1821
www.hummingbirdpresspoetry.com

Printed in Canada

*For Lisa Griest
and
Karin Connors*

Who always believed

And

*For my favorite "poems"
Rachael
Gabrielle
Simon
and
Quillan*

ACKNOWLEDGEMENTS

To the wondrous Stuart Smith, who refused to flinch in the face of my less than flattering artistic-temperament tantrums, but carried on with grace, good humor and perfect equanimity, I offer the "Editor's Red Badge of Courage," undying gratitude, and all my heart.

To Joseph McNeilly, who dragged me into this project: You are forgiven! Special thanks: It never would have happened without you!

To George Lober and Ken Weisner, who knew me in another incarnation: I am so thankful to once again experience your enthusiasm, enduring support and wonderful company. To newer friends Joanna Martin, Debra Spencer, Tilly Shaw, Tamara Wagner and Julia Alter: huge appreciation for your patience, kindness and generosity on my behalf, and special thanks to Julia Alter for not revealing my true identity to the poetry police.

Blessings to Joy O'Neal and her family, particularly to Alexis, who taught me the healing properties of poetry. And eternal gratitude to Len Anderson for all his work to make this book a reality. I am forever indebted.

Further appreciation to Joseph Stroud for his fine critique; Carter Wilson, an early inspiration; Dennis Morton who always made me laugh in class; and Karen James who always makes me laugh at work. Grand thanks to Jeanne Czarnecki and Burgundi Thureockes for listening to my incessant whining; and Shirli McLaughlin and The Third Hand Store for keeping me in the finest of finery—no slovenly writer, I.

To Sandra England whose painting graces both the cover of my book, and now my wall as well, I am honored to use your talent on my behalf. Many thanks. And of course to my parents, Dick and Louise Johnson, the world's biggest braggarts, all my love.

CONTENTS

Disclaimer	10
Learning the Dead Man's Float	13
The Lie of the Land	15
Learning the Dead Man's Float	17
The Distance Between Stars	19
Living with Icarus	20
Last Supper	21
Runaway	22
Living in the Ice House	23
Lamentation for My Son	25
Editing the Dead Languages: A Cautionary Tale	26
Message	28
Crippled	30
To Dream That One's Teeth Are Knocked Out	31
In the Shame Clinic	33
The Man Who Thinks He's Made of Glass	35
Fear of the Dark	36
On the Darkest Night of the Soul We Have a Pillow Fight	37
Untitled	38
Stilt Walking at Midnight	41
Lot's Wife	43
Stilt Walking at Midnight	44
Horse Prayers	45
Love Song and a Parade	46
Edgar in Sonogram	48
Epiphany	49
Cora's Choice	50
Eating the Walls: A Defense	51
Jesus Christ Resurrected as 20th Century Single Mother	53
Griffin	54

Bucks	55
What the Dawn Steals	56
Elegy for Angels	57
Benediction	58
In That House	60
The Hunter	61
Horse's Head	62
Seventh Summer	64
Snow Geese on June Lake	66
Killing Snakes	67
The Same Old Story	69
For China L. Who Died Because No One Would Hear	71
On the Night of My Son's Birthday the Bombs Begin to Fall	73

Circus Acts & Other Frolics   75

Driving into Albuquerque at Night	77
When the Circus Comes to Town	78
Big Top Soap Opera	79
Abracadabra	80
Learning Alchemy	82
In the House of Mirrors the Deaf Mutes Sing,	83
The Trapeze Artist Speaks	84
On Bowling Night the Fat Men Dance	85
Party Games	86
Observing the Eclipse	88
Spring	89
On Viewing Millais' *Ophelia*	90
Night Herons on Loch Lomond	91
Out of Left Field	92
When the Morning Stars Sing Together	93
Wonder	94
Blessed by the Myopic	96
The Soul Leaves the Body	98

*And if you wanted to drown, you could.
But you don't, because finally, after all
this struggle and all these years,
you don't want to anymore.
You've simply had enough of drowning
and you want to live, and you want to love.*
           David Whyte

Disclaimer
with apologies to W.C.W

A poem could be a dangerous country.
You might not want to go there.

Or if you do, find a guide, make sure all your papers are in order.
Things could happen there. Nothing is
predictable. Consider the weather: One minute all hot
and bothered, the next the whole world enveloped in
a sentimental mist and those famous sandy beaches
strewn with more broken hearts
than seashells tossed up after a tsunami.

An acquaintance, a hard man who insisted he had no
soft hues on his palette, who believed himself a brave
and brawny fellow, ventured there, full of disdain and
without trepidation. When he returned
he was weeping and did not stop for months. Every
afternoon, his lover said, he would bring a dozen
roses and lay them at her feet. Like a dog, she said,
delivering the daily paper.

A woman who read a misleading brochure, and
anticipating a luxurious vacation, imagined
hammocks, tall drinks of unlikely color stuffed with tropical blooms,
and perhaps a midnight serenade, arrived to find her
hotel overbooked and herself relegated to an
ENORMOUS shoe with a harried concierge and
flocks of small children
running up and down the halls at all hours of the day and night.

Then there is the story of the famed physician who
paid a visit and never returned.
Though now and then, his wife received odd and
beautiful messages scribbled on a prescription pad.
And once a crate of unusual souvenirs:

    A red wheelbarrow,

    A luminous stone shaped like a tear,
labeled

    GLAZED RAIN

    And a pair of white chickens

the Customs house never would release.

Learning the Dead Man's Float

The Lie of the Land

You cannot gauge the lie
of the land. It is angular, convoluted,
disjointed as an arm twisted
behind your back. It juts out
in unexpected places. The names
he murmurs in the dark are nowhere
on the map he has given you,
and the fine needle of your compass circles,

circles like something wild searching
for a scent. You rifle through your memory
trying to recall the final landmark.
Where was it? How many miles
back? How many miles to the moment
he last touched you, held you close enough
to feel the heat of your bones, yearning?
How many miles to now,

this wilderness without referents?
Even the Northern star conspires;
illuminates the quick-sly
glance of women on the streets,
a rendezvous wink,
the harsh glint of a sudden desire.

You cannot survey the lie
of the land. The terrain is treacherous.
There are chasms of shame
no sextant could measure. Lost,
you settle in. You gather up tinder and
camp there in the region of his deceit, waiting.

Though when he comes to you,
when he lies with you,
when he lies, right there in your arms,
still you are surprised.
Amazed to find he is weightless,
and glimmers
like a mirage on the furthest horizon.

Learning the Dead Man's Float

Stop struggling.
Don't wrestle this deep sadness
like Jacob's relentless angel
that would hold your head beneath the
surface of the water,
that would force you to inhale
every tear,
leave you gagging and sprawled,
dislocated on the ruined landscape
of your life.

Stop asking
the impossible questions:

Why did no one teach you how to swim?
Where is the bottom of this bottomless grief?

Stop struggling.

Belly down and grow gills.

Learn from the fishes.

Learn from the owl fish,
whose eyes are round and
radiant as Marie Curie's glowing platters.

From the giant red mysid,
who transforms terror, like an alchemist,
into clouds of opalescent snow.

Read the message from the sea pens,
scribbling like sparklers
across the inky black.

Learn from the lantern fish
the way that light can thrive
even in the darkest dark.

One day, one night,
you will roll onto your back,
and you will not differentiate
between blue of sea, blue of sky.

Between the constellations
in this luminous water,
the fiery pinpoints in that overhead night.

The Distance Between Stars

This August night, when the skies of summer loosen
and begin to fall,
we lay our bodies down
in the asphalt dark
and await the arc light of shooting stars.

Beside me, you name Orion, Pegasus, the lesser bear,
and then, the slow telling
of that terrible moment
you were hurled from the orbit
of your own life

…how your heart burst into a galaxy
of pain…how you drift there still…
like some abandoned cosmonaut cut loose
and left to float
in the private infinitudes of that grief.

Later, you will point out two stars
nestled on the night's horizon
and explain, how despite all appearances
they might be billions of light years
apart…
and I will not reach to touch you.

Already I know how far
a light year might be—

Living with Icarus

The way I sleep
against you.
The way I press my palms,
the left, the right
against the boned blades of your back.
Press them hard
against the places
where wings might explode.

The way I keep my vigil.
Have hidden away
the feather bed.
Burned the comforter,
the brimful pillows of down.
The way I count the candles,
as another might count
the candlesticks, the antique silver spoons.

The way I listen.
Cup my ear to the arc
of your chest and hear small muscles
mutate, the rustle and sigh
of something about to unfurl.
Already your bones have grown thin
as twigs; hollowed flutes where the wind
will begin to sing.

The way it will happen.
How one day I will waken
to a bed as empty and wide
as the tide-swept sand, will run
to the open window, gulls screeling
over stark water, and find nothing.
The way I will weep
the way that I weep.

Last Supper
> *One can't build little white picket fences to keep nightmares out.* —Anne Sexton

Do this:
Press your ear against the stove
and hear the singing.
There are canticles. And something else,
a secret murmur that implores you
to kneel on the linoleum,
open wide the oven door
and call.
Call your mother. Call your children.
Call the names of all the men you ever believed
might love you.
This is your confessional, this is your confession:

That you no longer believe.
That you've lost your faith in electroplated icons,
the silvered saints of toasters, metaled mixing bowls,
electrical knives.
That your prayers remain unanswered
though daily you bow before a sink
of dirty dishes. That you can't make meaning
from a matched set.
That you are lonely.

You cannot find solace in the shopping channel,
in the prayers of appliances whirring.
You are a woman who has come to understand
that KENMORE is truly less.
A woman seeking absolution with her head
in the oven.
Serving up her soul like a supper.

Runaway

One night you discover your daughter
poring over the creased map of your life
and in the morning even before you awaken
she is gone
roaring down the road
like every horse-powered auto ad
cliché her hair
a golden braid of sunlight
unraveling behind
ahead the purple highway
unspooling
the implication: her whole life before her

and that map, *your* map
unfolded in her lap
and all you can do is fall
on your knees and pray
for boil over
for blow out
for anything to slow her
send her calling from a roadside phone
so you can tell her
NO! *That map is all wrong!*
The cartographer a madman,
every road a dead end!

That whole world flat!

But she is speeding
toward the edge
and you cannot stop her.
You cannot stop her!

Living in the Ice House

I
The weather in this house
is not kind.
You could never call it
temperate
and to mention balmy
would be impossibly cruel.

It is not at all what we expected!

There are words we'd like to shout,
words bitter and despairing
as this air.
As difficult to swallow.
But we've heard the warnings:
        Avalanches are imminent!

II
We've sacrificed the hearts
of a hundred oaks,
offered up the limbs of willow,
hawthorn and hemlock to our hearth.
The furniture is long since
ashes, and the pictures hang
on the walls, forsaken without frames.
        We've burned everything.

But still we are trembling!

Where is the dog with his brandy? you say.
Who has hidden our heaviest quilts?

III
Once we were optimistic.
I dreamed coal-walkers, fire eaters.
You installed smoke alarms and sprinklers
on the ceiling.
Spontaneous combustion was always a possibility.
Now there is no tinder between us.

Now we have nothing.

        Not even two sticks to rub together.

Lamentation for My Son

Child,
I would build you a shelter
with my bones,
would mix the mortar from my own marrow,
from my own blood,
if I could give you refuge.

No child should live in the fallout
of love's difficult demise

but already I see that you wear our grief
in the sorrowing curve of your spine,
in the soles of your feet stepping
softly as shadow
so you will not be heard.

Beneath the weight of our rage, our shame,
you are growing smaller.

Child,
I would bandage your wounds
with my body,
would offer you the solace
of my own skin.
I would award you with ten Purple Hearts
if only I could heal

that *one*
we have so casually broken.

Editing the Dead Languages: A Cautionary Tale

Because
he was so easily bored
he left his placid lover and hung his hat
on the edge of an active volcano
where eruptions were imminent
and even the difficult air
exciting to breathe.

Nights,
he lay below the star-sparked sky and learned to sing
in a tropical tongue
for which there is no accurate translation.
The vowels, mysterious consonants, rolling
rich against the roof of his mouth like pieces
of a foreign fruit.
He swallowed phrases whole,
became fat and sated.

Under the influence of the casaba moon
he was proud to be so fluent, sent postcards
like flaming arrows
proclaiming his contentment.

He had forgotten his mother tongue.
Forgotten how a word might fall sudden and sharp
as cinder, burn through any kind of satisfied.

Though one day, that roiling in his belly,
the stench of dreams combusting.
One morning upon waking—the taste of sulfur.
Familiar ashes settled on his fevered lips.

Soon he will pack up his books,
unroll his maps and move on.
Hunt a new territory, seek a sparser vocabulary
with sentences untrammeled by such words as *history*,
or *hearth*
or *home*.

Message

Every night I stand at the border
and call your name into that country.
I know you are there.
I have heard the music of your guitar
and once your voice, speaking
in a foreign tongue.
Though I listened long in that darkness
I couldn't understand.

Always, I bring my offerings:
photos of our children, lock of hair,
a note you once wrote,
and pin them to the concertina wire.
In the moonlight they flutter, resemble
small white flags signaling
surrender against the night.
You do not answer.

If you could hear me
I would tell you
you have chosen your own exile,
but we are the displaced,
the disinherited, abandoned
amid the wrack of
your restless need.

I would tell you
that we are hungry.
That we have gnawed too long
the hard gristle of hope.
There is no sustenance left
in that splintered bone.

I would tell you
that I have heard the aching voices
of our children whisper prayers
across the border of a country
they have never seen.

Crippled

The skin carries its own memories,
murmurs all night, seeking
your absent body beneath the sheets
like a lost limb
accidentally severed.
I cannot sleep for the noise
and itch of it.
Or when I do, it is the wrenching
visions of desire,
the entanglement of arms and legs
wrapped around shadow.

Once I dreamed that you returned,
straddled my belly naked
and reaching down plucked out
the thinnest wishbone
like a sliver
from my chest.

Another night, you were a healer,
laid your hands on my wounds,
offered up the miracle of your fingers.
And for that moment, the flats of your palms
pressed hard on the arch of my solitude,
I was made whole.

It is the dawns I suffer most
when the seep of despair,
subtle as morning light, begins
its slow and insidious
crippling.

To Dream That One's Teeth Are Knocked Out

      denotes misfortune
      and a certain loss of power…

They spill out
    from your mouth
like polished tiles,
random pieces from a game
of Scrabble
    that you arrange
    and rearrange
shuffle
the sharp-edged letters
    of your teeth
backward
        forward
                across the tablecloth,

tongue spooling senseless syllables, and still

there are no words…

he has taken away the vowels!

He has taken away
        the vowels
and your PAIN
becomes PN, and your tears
are TRS
and how can you SCREAM
            or even BREATHE,
your throat clogged thick
with consonants?

How can you presume
even to exist
      without one solitary I?

In the Shame Clinic

Here, no one ever dreams of escape.

We are heavy.

Heavy-lidded, heavy-hearted,
hunkered down beneath the girders
of our histories.

We inhale shadows, and stagger,
crave the comfort of familiar sleep,
our intricate nightmares brocaded restraints.
We drowse on our sultry couches,
curl into corners,
suck our shame like black smoke
from an opium pipe.

Though
the doors are always flung wide;
the windows unbarred, no ceiling,
not even a roof, besides the seed-pearled night
or the flat-pressed day
that we rarely notice;

Though
our attendants are insistent,
incandescent as albinos,
as pale as the wild plum petals
that drift through the open ceiling,
land like a million winged insects,
on our spine-bent bodies;

Though
the doctors practice pointless levitation,
their pockets full of lithium and helium,
and the nurses, pinned to the floor
by their oxford soles, sing lullabies
of gossamer, thistle down,
sea foam;

We know a pipe dream when we see it.

Here, no one ever leaves.

Still, on occasion we are wakened
by a desperate weeping—
someone considering possibilities.

Someone dreaming again the impossible story
of the one they say ascended:
The one who hoarded hope in his heart
like pills in a dixie cup.
Who lifted up his head one day,
then his body; floated free from his slippers,
and laughing,
rose and drifted into the enormous,
dazzling sky.

> *The patient, suffering from a strange emotional disorder, perceives himself as exceptionally fragile. It's as if he thinks he's a pane of cheap thin glass.*   —World Weekly News

The Man Who Thinks He's Made of Glass

...sips Velvet Hammers and speaks
of a certain soprano.
"You've no idea," he says, "how I loved
and feared her—
the way she held me safe as bubble-wrap
between her breasts, those magnificent bellows.
I tell you, I couldn't imagine
a country softer than her flesh.

It was months before I discovered
tucked behind the trill of her tongue
she had a palate hard as diamonds!
The moment when she'd open
wide her throat
seeking out the highest C!
The purest pitch that shatters!
You understand, I had to leave her...."

He spreads his arms as wide as barricades across the bar.
"And people...they carry pebbles in their pockets
and sometimes something vicious as a stone.
It's all become so clear to me!
How our faces are brittle as crockery platters.
How our bones will snap like stemware
at the shrillest note.
How our souls are desolate spaces, the hinterland
inside blown glass.
How we are all broken...
How we are all broken men!"

Fear of the Dark

Or is it the implication of monsters
wrestling
underneath the bed,
the changeling behavior of coat racks
that disturbs you?

All night you keep a candle burning
and your night-light,
a globe illuminated at the poles:
the Arctic Circle,
Tierra Del Fuego.
Places you imagine without shadow
in their season.
Windswept,
absolute as ice.
Places where dreams require no interpretation.

You hold out your yellow lamp,
a talisman to ward off
the rustle behind the bureau,
the long familiar fingers
scraping at the sill.
But what you do not understand:
Light is the mother of shadow
and each of us carries our own darkness.
Even now it circles round your eyes
like something hungry.

If you turn your back
it will swallow you whole.

On the Darkest Night of the Soul
We Have a Pillow Fight

After all,
what else is there to do?
We've wrestled with shadows so long
we are sick
and slickened with sweat
and the whole room dank,
damp with stale tears.

It's pitch black in here
though we've burned all our bridges,
not a flicker, not even one coal
to see by.

Only this cloudburst
of black swan feathers raining down
on our heads
like ash.

Untitled

It is the names of the dead.
The names of the disappeared
etched on slivers of silver.
We carry that weight in our bones.

This is what we own together.
This is our unholy bond:

That we know the honed edge
of hope splintered,
the shock of dreams shattered,
lodged like shrapnel
cold beneath the ribs.

We are wounded tending to wounded.
Our bodies applied like a poultice,
warm flesh against flesh
to draw out the shards
twisting through tissue and skin.

It is the nights the ghosts speak,
we fever and tremble.

We know the pierce of memory wending
through muscle, through dream.
This is what we own together.

But this will be our holy bond:
that one morning we will waken
and recognize each other,
and slowly, so slowly
begin again to sing.

Stilt Walking at Midnight

Lot's Wife

His name is Mr. Lot
but the children call *"Hey Empty!"*
and run, giggling.

All day he squats in the open field,
hunched beside the salt-lick,
and weeps.

He is carving it into a beautiful woman.
It is his wife, he says.
"I can taste her," he says.
"She lives in my tears."

Each dawn, the simple-faced sheep gather.
They kiss Lot's wife good morning,
smoothing her curves
with their black and lovely tongues.

Stilt Walking at Midnight
for Rachael and Gabrielle

They falter,
balanced on their spindled legs
like white colts freshly unfolded
and learning to stand.

Or herons,
tilting high above milkweed and thistle,
each step a hesitation, a contemplation;
the way their cotton gowns ruffle,
plumage bleached pale
by this meadow moon.

These are the daughters of the town
come to practice the secret rituals
of rising.
Though even in this darkness
you can see it: how they bend
their faces earthward,
a certain yearning
underneath anticipation.

This is the way they believe it will be—
everything the same, but further
                              from reach.

Horse Prayers

Air travelers should avoid the early evening flights,
when skies are congested with something more fervent
than jets or thunderheads:
the ten thousand Invocations of prepubescent daughters
ascending.
The hours of the Horse Prayers.

Pious girls bow at mapled bedsteads,
their knees pressed hard as bribes
into the bedroom floor, beseeching
piebalds, palominos, a gentle canter.

Others, supine on flowered sheets,
stare at the ceiling, whinny sighs
like appeals into the atmosphere,
bidding the miracle
of hip against haunch.

Air travelers beware!
A desire this profound is dangerous!
Could bring down any pilot!
Could make the radar's needle
prance
and pitch!

Love Song and a Parade
for Simon

My son, who is a festival unto himself.
Who is a carnival.
Who is all three rings of the circus.

Who celebrates his teenaged body
like an unexpected gift,
all lank and limb.
Who marvels at his muscles in the mirror,
amazed,
amused
at what he is becoming.

He is becoming—
my son, who wears the curls upon his head
like a raucous bouquet of thistles
and thicket,
and is not abashed,
except before the girls too beautiful
to bear.

My son, who does not walk, but limbos,
frolics, jigs.
Who tangos from the shower in a towel.
Who does the tarantella to the table.
Who even in his sleep, waltzes the sorrowful mazurka,
entangles in the sheets and still
is never, ever, still.

My son, who does not speak, but sings!
Raves and rollicks, exclaims!
Proclaims all the world
a *Glorious* and *Grand* event!
Who is astonished, wonder-filled
by something mundane
as a man in brown trousers.
My son, who is wonder full.

My son, who is a festival unto himself.
Who is a carnival,
      a love song and a parade.

Edgar in Sonogram
for my grandson

We peer into your mother's belly
as if it were a crystal ball
            and you steal our breath!

We are seeing the future!

The back of your head round and thrilling
as a newly discovered planet,
your miniscule hands shooting like stars
through the humid dark.

Your mother complains.
All night, she says, you scritch and nick
and tap
and will not let her sleep,
and I imagine your nails,
minute slivers glittering like mica
in your unborn night
and scratching messages
from the other side.

What are you trying to tell us, Edgar?

Come soon!
Tell us everything you know!

Epiphany

At first, I have to admit, I am taken aback—
all that light emitting
from the top of your head,
your face
luminescent as a Las Vegas midnight…

I imagine freak accidents involving radium
or an unfortunate tangle
with Nikolai Tesla's infamous
transforming coil.

I think: *pyrotechnics*
I think: *incandescence*

It is Nothing
like Anything
I have ever seen.

You are blazing
—I can feel your heat at fifty paces–
and falling towards me like a star.

It's that moment
while I stand transfixed and waiting
for the strike of fire touching flesh,
that it comes to me:

It is you!
It is only you!
It is you
in all your light!

Cora's Choice
a birth poem

It was the night
they stood barefoot on the edge
of the wildest beach on the Barbary Coast,
their laughter
a tossed bouquet in the reveling surf,
the moon a strobe flash
through the bullying clouds,
their faces
made nacreous in that sudden light.

It was the night they stood astonished.

The night Neptune's mer-lambs came
romping from the tide,
their sea-foam wool phosphoresced
against the darkened sand.

Perhaps it was the wonder of that moment that called
to you, Cora.

Or perhaps you were already there
waiting to choose
the tallest, most elegant among them,
tugging at his cap
like a windsock,
to point the direction of his life.

Eating the Walls: A Defense

Pica: a perverted craving for substances unfit for food, as chalk, etc., symptomatic of certain diseases, and also occurring during pregnancy.
—Oxford English Dictionary

They say sometimes at night
the plaster fairly sings,
and I confess
I've heard it call.
The lure of rooms in Pink Parfait
and Mint
relentlessly demanding to be tasted.

And who to judge
who has not felt the tapiocaed texture
of stucco on the tongue,
the pure white cream of pasteboard,
smooth
and cool as icing.

This child would suck the marrow
from his own mother's bones
were he denied!

And yes it's true...
we pregnant women have been known
to eat the walls!
To tear them down with only nails
and teeth!
But we rebuild with teeth
and nails,
rows and rows of ribs
curving round the soul.

A weird maternal alchemy, admitted:
to transform firebrick and ash

to hanks of human hair
and flesh.
Yet how can you begrudge our appetites?
How can you withhold the chalk?

Don't you hear it singing in your bones?

Jesus Christ Resurrected as 20th Century Single Mother

Truth be told
you're not all that happy
to be back.
And already you can smell
three days' dirty dishes
moldering in the sink, and a mountain
of laundry piled higher than Mt. Sinai
by the hamper.

You'd like to lie here a little longer.
That business of dying was difficult,
exhausting, really took it out of you,
and you'd imagined something more
rewarding than a three day nap.
Perhaps a millennium. Maybe two.

But somebody's rooster is crowing
and crowing, and the baby is wailing
loud enough to wake the dead, and you sigh
and know it is time to cast off your sheets and
arise!
Though at first, it's almost too much!
The disaster of your house, the state
of the baby's diapers,
tempts you to shout your own full name
or fall to the carpet and cry
My God! My God! Why hast thou forsaken me?

Finally, it is the faces of your daughters,
tear-stained, startled from sleep,
smiles slow as sunrise
that make you understand:
Here are the miracles of grace.
Here is your redemption.

Griffin

The day you slid from my body
months too early,
and left your brother to fend for himself,

the white cat who patrolled the perimeter fence
turned black as mourning weeds.

And the crows, usually raucous and polished
in their night-oiled feathers,
turned somber and pale as milkweed and ash.

The world lost all its color,
Griffin,
the long day I held you,
tiny and cold.

That longest day I buried you deep
beneath the willow tree,
its limbs already bare,
its leaves already wept.

The winter months without color;
the flat white days,
the slate blank nights,
everything silhouette and shadow.

I grieved you, Griffin.

Until that final frosted morning,
when at last the first nibs burst
green on the willow branches
and I knew that your brother would come,
broad shouldered and struggling
to bear the weight of you both
into the on-rushing Spring.

Bucks
for Simon and for Ben

When they discover the doe still warm
by the side of the road and drag the body
home, rush to gather knives
and stones, they would slice the moon,
the stars from the skin of the sky,
they are so High And Mighty.
They are Warriors, fierce
and crouched, oblivious to blood,
the tug of tendon against blade,
until they split her wide
and find the fawns.

As if they have been struck—
the way they reel back then kneel over the bowl of her open belly

No longer fearsome hunters,
these are only small boys
who've not yet outgrown
their own dappled childhood.

Together, without speaking they lean
and lift out the fawns, first the one then the other,
still in their birth sacs, and lay them on the lawn,
like gifts waiting to be opened.
"Bucks," my son says, and his friend
holds that word in his mouth
for a solemn moment.

They look away then, across the empty lawn,
their eyes still wide and startled
like young deer caught in sudden bright
light and uncertain
                which way to leap.

What the Dawn Steals

Sometimes in the morning
you awaken startled and treading
dark water.
Sorrow has wrapped around your ankles
in the dawn and you are wearing
cement shoes.

You would like to climb aboard the body
of your lover,
clutch his sleeping shoulders
like a refugee
clinging to a raft,

but you know this kind of weight
would sink you both.

When you slept you dreamt
marvels and miracles:
your babies, long buried,
awake and nestled in your lap,
their faces shining up at you
luminescent as moons.

When you slept you spoke their names aloud.

When you slept you walked on the water.

Elegy For Angels
for my lost children

Oh! These angels have no intention of huddling on the head of a pin! They are far too rambunctious for a place pastel as heaven, prefer the primary clamor of my kitchen, where they hover above pots and pans, begging for tapioca, Dream Whip, white rice.

One has dipped his wing into the soup, and sits perched on the toaster solemnly preening.

Another finds fascination in the egg timer, twists the dial, tilts it to her ear like a cup pressed to the wall, listening to the murmurs from the other side, the small clicks of eternity ticking. While the baby nestles in the breadbox, round as a loaf, a fine sift of flour dusting her delicate wings.

The little one, barely a toddler and still clumsy in flight, is fond of the black-tongued parrot and is learning a filthy vocabulary. *Dirty dog!* he shrieks. *On your back you whoring wench!* He mimics like a miracle.

Though when I try to teach him the simple word of *Mama*, slipping syllables through the birdcage like an offering, he turns stubborn. Insistently mute or suddenly screeching in a voice as shrill as chalk: *Manna! Manna!* his small mouth working fiercely as a beak, and clutching a crust of bread in one pink fist.

We are fervent as yeast in this kitchen, until twilight spills heavy and dark as Original Sin, a stain that clings, drags them back to that limbo where they dangle upside-down like white bats or miscarried prayers.

Where they hang, head first and just out of reach, curled and fisted. Awaiting, like small poems, the moment to be born.

Benediction
for Raj

In Heaven, the preacher proclaims,
all the angels are male,
and the men
begin to rumble sweet and low
clutched inside their too-tight Sunday collars,

and so beautiful, he intones,
they don't require clothing!
and the women
quiver and fan, bulletins aflutter like a hundred frantic
wings beating beneath the steepled roof.

And she feels those words burn brimstone and fire,
sluice through her body
until she wants to sing it out like a hymn
Hallelujah! Hallelujah! Hallelujah!

***

All that summer she rides
her bike through the blank night,
pedaling her way through dark and desire, going
small-town nowhere, awaiting,

that moment, years later
when he stands before her for the first time,
naked, turned away,
and she can see the down-bladed bones
of his back, the pin feathers curling scapulae.

She whispers it then,
hallelujah, hallelujah, hallelujah

until he lays her down and quiets her
with his own hot mouth
against her skin.

In That House

The children have no tongues.
The Mother cuts them out
while the Father reads stern words
from the thick black book,
his voice a heavy hatchet falling onto bone.

Later she will gather
the tongues to her and hang them
from the highest branch of an orchard tree
like burnished chimes, to frighten away
the clamorous birds.

At night, the neighbors say,
there are hymns of Blood,
Wrath and Redemption. And sometimes,
when the wind is low, the wavering small voices
of the children, singing still.

Horse's Head

When first you see it you cannot say it,
and when you do say it
it stutters from your mouth
in a terrible Morse Code
that no one can decipher.
Your brothers smirk, your father stares,
your mother offers remedial mugs
of hot milk, the promise of bed,

but you stand resolute,
trembling, stupidly mute until
reluctantly they follow you back
into the icy dusk.

You need them to know what you cannot tell

how you stumbled there,
how it blazed
startling and white
as a meteor
beneath the black water,
the flannelled nostrils, the lashes,
the pleats of the muzzle
already rimmed with an etching of algae.
And the single eye, wide open
staring
up at you, the jaw
clenched tight…

Walking through the snow
you pass your own footprints
slurry in the setting sun and running
in the opposite direction,

and you know then
it will be too late,
that the thin skin of evening ice
will seal away the secret
that no one else will see.

Already your father stands bellowing
at the edge of the pond, his breath hanging
hot against the freezing air,
yelling—

> *There is nothing! Nothing there!*
> *And what kind of person would do that sort of thing?*
> *What kind of person would hack off a horse's head*
> *and throw it in a pond?! Tell me! What kind of person?!*

And you want to tell him

It is the kind of person
that held the hunting knife against
your own white throat
and made you promise never to speak
of the other things he had done
and would do
and would not stop.

The Hunter

He was the king of wounded things.
He carried them from the forest
to his fortress:
the pens of wood and wire he'd built
behind his father's house.

The blind fawn,
mute with fear, its eyes
pale as milk-glass.
A red-tailed hawk, still fierce
though both wings were shattered
and matted with blood.
Twin hares huddled in the corner,
their long hind legs slit
at the tendons, limp and useless
as empty furred gloves.
The snarling coyote, yellow-eyed, feverish,
unable to rise on its splintered paw, and slowly starving.

As if seeking absolution.
As if remorse could heal.
His angry hands,
momentarily gentled, cleaned the wounds,
changed the dressings.
His own voice raised in a desperate keening
to quell their yowls and whimpers—
to silence those other raging voices
commanding him over and over,
Gather your rifle, your whetted knife.
Begin again that terrible march
into the shivering,
the waiting,
woods.

Seventh Summer

All that summer I lived in a rowboat
and hid in tulles
taller than a man.
Taller than you.

And I began
to learn the hard lessons.

To interpret the lap of the lake
against smooth stone.
To read the code of cattails
rustling.
The red-tipped warning
of the blackbird's wing.

From the water snake I learned
protective coloration.
My hair bleached pale as rushes,
my eyes turning umber
as lake-bottom silt.

Flat in the bow of my splintering boat
I was translucent as lake light.

Though never did I venture
into the open waters.
The dark shafts of sun
where you set your father's decoys.

Already I had learned
better than the bittern,
better than the mallard,
to scent a predator.

Already I knew you were waiting
crouched and hungry just behind the blind.

Snow Geese on June Lake

How can I tell you what I saw
when I returned to that place?
How can I explain those stumps
frozen fast in the lake's dark ice?
Legs seeping blood,
without bodies,
like stubble left in the field
after a vicious harvest.

Or how I skated
carving desperate figure 8's
around those feet webbed into the ice
and glistening like rinds
of cast-off Christmas fruit.

They must have believed he was some kind of Savior.
The way he walked on water
in his thick-soled boots.
They must have believed it was Salvation
he carried, wooden handled
and shining
in his hands.

As I tried to believe
that perhaps they'd flown away.
Grown tired of the need to stand or walk.
Absolved themselves of the awkward burden
of feet that could never outrun
the bitterest bite,
the unforgiving slash of the axe.

Killing Snakes

You are the shooter.
I gather up the corpses
quickly, you are so insistent
with the tip of your polished new gun.

In fairy tales there would be berries
in this basket, weighing heavy as a wound
against the crook of my arm, blue veined.
And the juice would run sweet
between my fingers.

In fairy tales there would be possibilities:
A frog prince when you slit the belly.
A golden egg. A fleck of moonstone tucked
among the scales, faint as hope—
something to believe in.

I do not believe. Have not believed,
though you load each word
with the significance of whispers,
the way you load your gun.

Demanding drama.
Demanding some small terror
when you drape the snakes across my barely
budded breasts, wrap them writhing round my wrists,
my waist, my ankles.

You force this flesh upon me like a gag,
relentless in your ritual, your myth.
They claim a wounded snake will turn,
twist upon itself and bite twenty times
or more to die.
But this is not a story you relate.

In fairy tales this blood would rise,
travel into forked tongues and shriek.
And your remorse would seek you sharp as poison.
In fairy tales I'd shed the memory of your touch,
shake you loose as easily as rotting skin.

The Same Old Story

Chapter I
She believed differently.

She had forgotten
how it could adhere
on the underside of muscle. Invisible.
A rogue cell hiding out for years.

She thought she had rubbed that rage away
when she rubbed the backs of her babies,
who had come so quickly there was no time
for memory.
She thought that no memory meant no history.

That is where she made her mistake.

Chapter II
The genetics of love are impossible to trace.
There are no markers.

She would have disagreed.
She would have argued otherwise.
The way love weaves through DNA
is a knot work, she'd say,
too complicated to untangle.

Chapter III
She speaks like an amnesiac unraveling a nightmare.

She tells it as if it were someone else.
Those girls she calls them, though anyone could see—
the cock of the hip, the disposition of shoulders,
these are her blood daughters.

Chapter IV
How she went there as if she still believed
she could offer some kind of shelter.

How she pushed them apart, the one
battering the other from some private storm,
the other beaten down, already wailing.

How when it came to her,
it came like fire,
the hard burn of her own history snapping,
tightening the tendons of her forearms.

Afterword
How she understood at that moment
there was nothing at all between them
but her own fists
upraised like an ugly fence.

For China L. Who Died Because No One Would Hear

I.
Because no one would hear,
it is best that you are deaf
and mute.
The bones of words are brittle,
would surely snap
beneath the weight of your telling.

And what to tell
that is not spoken in the
thousand blue tongues tattooed
across your face, your arms and breasts,
his signature.
And what to hear
more terrible than the rise
and swell of your own
strangled scream.

In darkness you trace
the wounds with fingertips,
read your welts like Braille,
seeking light beneath the blood.
Light that twists to torment
in the morning mirror.
Light that mocks your vision.
Deaf, mute, you yearn
for the relief, the pure and colorless
dark of the absolutely blind.

II
Next door, neighbors pretend.
Pretend deaf,
dumb,
blind.
Pretend ignorance.

Pretend not to understand the Sign
of slaps and shoves,
though it's a simple language,
without nuance.
A language clear as a fist.

On the streets they shun you.
You are a shame,
your blackened eyes a reproach.
(You must've misbehaved.)
And it's obvious;
you will not hold out
your empty cup.
You do not beg.
And how can they forgive you,
if you refuse to beg?
You're a slap in the face
of all that is good
and kind
and decent.

III
He's a good man, they say.
A kind and gentle man.
He cares for her, they say.
He gives her things.
These are the things he gives her:
He gives her a piece of his mind.
He gives her the back of his hand.
He gives her colors.
Every shade of purple,
livid reds, pinks, deepest blues.
Hideous greens
and yellows too garish to wear
outside the house.
And once he gave her roses.

On the Night of My Son's Birthday the Bombs Begin to Fall
for Quillan

On the night of my son's birthday
the bombs begin to fall
on Baghdad.

Begin to fall
on other children
who might be dreaming in their beds
of parties and birthdays.
Who might awaken and imagine
for an instant
that this show of fireworks
shattering the sky
is their own astonishing celebration.

And I consider how my own son
might also imagine
that these candles we hold high
nationwide in our vigil
are a million birthday candles.

And he would not be mistaken.

We hold these tiny flames aloft
guarded in our hands
for every child's birthday.
And we pray that they burn bright,
that they do not flicker.

We pray that they not be snuffed out.

Circus Acts & Other Frolics

Driving into Albuquerque at Night

down
into that great bowl of light
and the liquid white traffic
      pouring in
           too fast
                spilling
                      over the edges
and the sky spattered
with stars
as if the SPLASH
of all that light
      has spackled the walls
           and ceiling
                of the night

When the Circus Comes to Town

How the town boys burn
for the fire-eater's flame-haired daughter.
How they moth against her, flurry around her
so eager to singe their foolish unfurled hearts.
All afternoon they practice their secret stunts,
the price of admission
to step inside the flaps of her tent.

One breaks an ankle attempting to balance
on the backyard clothesline.
One breaks the Sunday china and slices a hand
in a juggling mishap.
Yet another, for lack of a lion, presses his head into
the jaws
of a neighbor's bull mastiff and requires several
firemen
and stitches.

All over town love's casualties . . .

And the fire-eater's flame-haired daughter
lies napping in the arms of her gypsy bare-back rider,
and never awakens to the sirens
or dreams of the small fires
burning all around her.

Big Top Soap Opera

The night the magician disappeared
with the sword-swallower's wife . . .

The night the sword-swallower tasted
his sharpest blade, so as never to speak her name . . .

The night the fortune-teller, who'd always known,
laid down her cards and crossed herself twice . . .

The night the stars teetered in the sky,
tenuous tight rope walkers stumbling in the dark . . .

The night the crescent moon somersaulted,
hung like the down-turned mouth of the sad-eyed clowns . . .

The night the fat lady opened her arms wide
to the melancholy arias and began to sing . . .

Abracadabra

> *The magician must always do two things at once...He is telling one story, while thinking another, therein lies the charm of magic.*
> —Harry Blackstone

Act I — The White Lies

He flips them from his magic hat
like rabbits.
They scuttle and skid across your floor,
twitching.
You tell yourself: They're harmless.
You tell yourself: These are only illusions for my amusement.
Later they will gnaw.
Even now, the big one, the one in the corner
with eyes as red as radicchio,
is beginning to burrow a nest
in the softest tissues around your heart.

Act II — Tricks Without Mirrors

When you ask him
and he opens his palms to you,
they are empty. Seamless as gloves.
He offers no clues.
Though with the others
he pulls flamboyant histories from thin air,
knotted,
slippery as scarves,
proffers silver coins from up his sleeves,
and once a dove
released from the thicket of a woman's pale hair.
It flies to the ceiling,
batters a weak applause against the rafters.

You wonder
who will be there to clap
when it is your turn to vanish?

Act III — Finale

He calls you his helpmate.
His loyal assistant.
He says he depends on you
for all his deceptions.
Soon he will ask you to lie flat
in his big black box.
Soon he will stand above you
delicately fingering the razor teeth
of his newly sharpened
saw.

Learning Alchemy

The woman who sleeps with Siamese twins
loves only one and detests the other
who stinks of Muscatel
and makes his brother drunk against his will.
Who slurs her name from the farthest side of the bed.
Who slurs her,
calls her fickle.
Calls her a woman who does not know
where love leaves off
and hate begins.

She listens in the oily dark
and is amazed to hear
how the alchemy of anger can transmute
the soft lead of consonants
and vowels
into something sharp enough
to slash her
wide apart.

In the morning
over sterile breakfast linen she will practice
this new-found sorcery.
Sickle,
she will tell them.
Skill saw.
Guillotine.
Her voice hard as surgical steel,
slicing
and deft as a scalpel.

In the House of Mirrors the Deaf-Mutes Sing,

their hands raised
like an infinitude of voices,
their white fingers in the looking glass
grown suddenly long
and graceful as the throats of swans.

How they sing!

A woman in gingham
lifts her arms like curly willow limbs,
weaves an undulated ballad
while a girl delighted
with the concave mirror
bebops and scats with staccatoed
thumbs and fingers
and her brother belts out
a wild yodel with jubilant palms.

How they stir the air with their songs!

Their metacarpal melodies waft
into the midway,
rise like a helium bouquet
into the circus night.

The Trapeze Artist Speaks

"When we were babies
she'd hang us out
like scraps of wind on the backyard line
and we'd doze there in the sun
lullabyed by the song of laundry flapping.

Later, our father would lift us high,
let us wrap our arms and legs around
the knotted pine rafters, leave us dangling
bent-kneed and bespangled
like glittering bats, roosting.

Each summer, a new swing
looped around the sickle moon.
Each winter, the Northern Lights
our blazing tent. The whole shining sky
our palaestra.

We were the lucky ones.
Not like the clown children—
pie-faced, baggy-pantsed, condemned to trip
round and round the dusty ring.
Perpetually grounded in clod hopper shoes.

We didn't need shoes…

We walked on the air!

We shot from the cannons to the very tip
top of the Big Top,
the crowd below
a universe of ooohs and ahhhs.

We never ever used a net!"

On Bowling Night the Fat Men Dance

On bowling night the fat men dance
in party shoes
and colored shirts inscribed with names
their mothers never dreamed of—Biff and Rocko
and Pinky—
while cocktail girls teeter
beneath trays of Bud
and dyed bouffants,
incendiary red
and twice the height of the Sears Chicago Tower.
It's a modern day miracle they do not topple!

Or perhaps a gravity overload...

already holding down at least a hundred
bowling balls,
snatching back the flying pins,
the flailing arms,
the laughter, BIG, BOISTEROUS,
heavy as Puccini—
who would be surprised
that these gigantic men could do the tarantella?
Or that something light as hair
could point the way to heaven?
Who would be surprised to know
the parking lot has lifted, whirling
vacant
and weightless as the night?

Party Games

Musical Chairs

Once again the music
    STOPS!
And all the chairs are taken!

Still you whirl from seat
to seat propelled
by disbelief. Your party dress,
your pointy hat, your patent leather shoes
impossible to halt!

Bobbing for Apples

From the bucket they beckon,
inviting Valentines.
You dip your face into the icy water
—they elude you.
The way the heart of the boy
you have always desired
eludes you.

Your arms are tied behind your back,
your eyes are wet,
your mouth. You might as well weep
for those bright red promises
you can never
ever taste.

Pin the Tail on the Donkey

Outside the sudden midnight of your blindfold
directions fly bright as confetti.
You spin away
       and stagger,
              stabbing your tack
                      again and again
                              into brilliant air.

Observing the Eclipse

I
Polish up your patent leather shoes
and put them here
beneath my dress. But
do not touch my skirt,
though your hands ache to lift it.
Remember the danger, the warnings:

NEVER LOOK WITH THE NAKED EYE!

You must be contented with
the tiny pin-hole projection
on the shining tips of your toes.
Do you see it?
Do you see the pearly pink
corona?
Do you see Bailey's Beads
glistening?

II
When I open my thighs
animals grow disturbed, birds
fly to roost, and old women clutching rosaries
press children to the dark musk
of their skirts.
Horses have been known to stampede.

And somewhere a blind man stands
smiling at a memory the black discs of his glasses
will never disclose.

Spring

It's Spring!
And the Sirens are singing
from the *Hormone Hotel!*
Can't you hear them calling?

They know your name
in fifty different languages:
from the balconies, they beckon.
"*Zuccherino mio! Mon petit chou chou!*"

They are begging your attentions.
Don't be stingy!
Go! And let them teach you
the secret dances of desire,
the tangled tangos, the wanton waltzes,
the hundred and three ways
one body can move
beneath another.

I'm telling you, it's Spring!
Unstop the winter wax
from your ears. Wake up!
Hear the Sirens singing!

On Viewing Millais' *Ophelia*

To do the back-float it is important
to relax
to dream
with eyes half-open
what is light:
> *The bones of birds*
> *Galileo's pound of feathers*
> *The pure white shell of an egg*
> *Or the petal of a lily.*

To lie across the water
flat as a reflection
balanced only on the backs
of the little fishes.

Night Herons on Loch Lomond
for David

They are so bored, these sentinels
relegated to this farthest finger of the lake
like God's own dark angels posted
at the gates of Paradise.

This paradise where no one bothers to venture.
This backwater, these tattered guardians
half-molted, perched
stiff legged on rotting stumps.

Only the fierce red coal of their eyes,
the scissored blades of their beaks,
belie the ancient memory of flaming swords flashing
across the garden.

One of them preens apathetically.
The other, head bowed over its own reflection,
peers into the lake and prays
for something exquisite,

something delicate as an opalescent dragonfly,
or perhaps the tasty underbelly
of an emerald-gilded
water frog.

Out of Left Field

So where exactly is it,
this weed patch so crop-full of bitter surprises
that we never
ever
see coming?

As if from some parallel universe,
filled with malevolent farm hands flinging
refuse from their furrows:
rotted cabbages, the random stone,
raining down upon our stupefied heads.

And why this stiff-necked insistence?
Our *right* turn only!
The *right* to this! The *right* to that!
So that we never ever heed
that lesson taught at every mother's knee:
> *Stop at the curb.*
> *Look both directions*
> *before stepping into the busy street!*

When the Morning Stars Sing Together
—Job 38:7

All along the road tonight the dogs are howling;
a certain sign
the constellations have begun to sing.
Like a choir of celestial mutes, their voices ring
in an unearthly pitch privy only to angels
and dogs.

Dogs, who hide disguised beneath the fine-furred
flaps of their ears, the most delicate drums;
miniscule radar dishes especially ordained
to receive the astral arias
of stellar sopranos—
they are the most blessed of beasts.

Be still!
Don't rush out to shut them up!
Go quietly instead,
and tilt back your head to the skies.
Listen to the dog songs.
Their muzzles are megaphones
for the stars.

for my mother, who taught me

Wonder

Say you are a farmer in Nebraska.
Say your life is every word for the color brown.
Say that daily you squat dust spackled
with the other men,
speak of topsoil, subsoil, the million subtleties
of dirt. You sift it through your fingers
watch it fall, think sepia, umber, rich sienna.
When you speak of the sky, you say blue.

Say one night, one day, a terrible wind . . .
Suspend your disbelief here and say it lifts you,
like in a bad B movie, tractor and all
and whirls you away, thumps you down days/
hours later in an unploughed field
on the pitched edge of the California coast.
You recognize the soil,

the same loam as your Nebraska earth.
But nothing else familiar. Not these burnished cliffs.
Not that roiling sea below, or the frenetic sky
one minute Wedgwood, suddenly cerulean
then twisting into colors
you cannot name.
A world in perpetual motion
as if to impress on the flat horizon of your mind

the unfathomable fact: the earth is a spinning globe
and you are perched precariously,
dizzied with wonder.

And how can you plough one straight furrow
above these cliffs where every meridian kinks
serpentine across the land?

Or sit atop your tractor and resist
plunging
right over the edge into that magnificent,
unmowed verdant field?

Blessed Be the Myopic

Blessed be the myopic
in the morning
for who else among you
could name the mirror
at six a.m. a friend,

or believe the pile of clothes
discarded last night on a chair
is this morning a secret
admirer, hastily dressed
and too shy to speak.

Even the kitchen is kinder:
The sharp-edged counter tops
a blur, the stove benign
as buttermilk, the unmopped
spills shimmering mirages
on the table.

Blessed be the myopic
in the morning,
who stumbles
on the obvious,
but wanders not
through that famous Vale of Tears,
who sees the light,
even the air,
through veils,
like Isadora Duncan
dancing.

Exalt, you myopic
and praise the merciful God
who bestowed on you
the vision
of moles.
Give praise!
Lift your glasses high!

The Soul Leaves the Body

And You!

You stand there arms akimbo,
yelling your commands *Come! Sit! Stay!*

down the empty street.

This is not the language of the soul.
You must learn a new vocabulary,

speak in the tongues of a softer palate.

You must learn to say *Dance.*
You must learn to say *Sing.*

You must learn

to throw *Joy* into the air
like a stick.

Jonell Esmé Jel'enedra has been a field hand, soda jerk, book reviewer, waitress, ditch digger, schoolteacher, sales clerk, and used clothing pricer. Currently she is a mother of four, occasional poet, and library employee. She holds a degree in Aesthetic Studies from UC Santa Cruz, which qualifies her to make sweeping judgments about the nature of beauty in the world. She has been published in *Ally*, *Quarry West*, *Writing for Our Lives*, *Porter Gulch Review*, *The Bathyspheric Review*, and several anthologies. She is a winner of a Mary Lonnberg Smith Award and the *Quarry West* Poetry Award, First Prize, 1999. She lives in Santa Cruz, California.